Odewale Saheed Ayinde

The success comes to those who burn their bridges

ISBN 978-1-312-69494-1

This book is for ambitious people who want to get ahead faster. The book will explain what is meant by burning your bridge. It also discusses the stories of successful men who burned their bridges for success. It explains the never burn bridge myth and how to cross the bridge before burning. One of the most important aspects of this book is the emphasis given to negative effect of having option and the benefit to be derived from burning your bridge.

TABLE OF CONTENT

CHAPTERS

INTRODUCTION

Success and life is all about having goals and the motivation behind them in order to make them happen. The two go hand in hand, it's about the passion and hard work you put into something and eventually get an output. It is the discipline set for you self and for what you is doing to make sure that you are always challenging yourself and going way above and beyond your limit.

Clarity of knowing what you are doing and how you are going to do it. Not just simple wishes and goals. It's your action that plan on you setting forth. It is about what you are going to do to make this walk a reality. There should not be any ifs in your goal setting. Don't think of a goal as a wish, but rather your future self and the position you plan on putting yourself in.

Sure it sound a bit cocky and over confident but confidence is well needed for what you plan on pulling off in your life. The issue is that most people view goal setting as a wish or as a fairytale rather than a course of action that needs to be taken. We usually look at a goal or something we wish to attain but not as something we are going to accomplish. It is a hope not a forgone.

Once you make promise to your self of never turning back to your old life and moving forward on your goal, there is no fail safe net to catch you, nor a plan B. it's just having your eyes on the target and knowing what your target actually is.

CHAPTER ONE

WHAT IS BRIDGE BURNING?

Creating that harmony starts with knowing exactly what you want out of life. Design the life you want in your mind. Be sure of it. Then discard all other options. It is either you will have the life or you will not live at all. It is either you will succeed at getting what you truly want in life or you will die trying all the days of your life. Do not settle for anything that is less. Coming up with an alternative life will not and should not do. Yes, you may need to rework the route to your ultimate desire every now and then, but never change the destination. The bridge I'm talking about isn't relationship we need to let go of in order to succeed, although many of us have them. These bridges are the safety net's we all have in case we fail. They are the backup plan. The plan B' we map out incase of our business venture is a complete failure. In case the road we've embrace on is tougher than we originally thought.

Do not say to yourself "I will try to be a great singer and if that fails then I will try teaching" such light hearted decisions rarely bear lasting fruits. Decide to be a singer, if that is your passion in life, and stick to it relentlessly. Having options makes you lazy. Having options make you unfocused and undetermined.

The bridge are the options will have incase of target goes tougher. We need to let go of those bridges to secede. They are holding us back as they are the safety nets we all have just in case shits hit s our fan. They are the action to keep us floating by.

Successful people don't have bridges to plan B because that just shows they are confident with their plan B. your goal should always be to get plan A done and executed the way you intended. One you stop and move on to plan B and cross that bridge, you have given up on your self and you hope to achieve your goal.

The phrase “if anything” or worse case scenario” “may be” shouldn’t exist in your vocabulary. A bridge is something you will find missing in the plan of your heroes and successful people through out history. Where we differ from them, is that their eventual success was a forgone conclusion. Where ours is a dream, a wish, and a blessing if it ever is recited for them, the Edwin C. Barnes and Thomas Edison, of the world, it was a matter of when not if. If they fail one, they would try a second time, and a third time, fourth and fifth. Thomas Edison had more than 10,000 failures before creating the light bulb. How many times are you willing to fail before you succeed? Thomas Edison didn’t go to his plan B or cross back over to the bridge, he kept going forward and that is what success is al about.

The reality is that most people are not willing to risk losing their comfortable life they have set up for themselves to attain something greater and something that they will actually enjoy having rather than being miserable. People acknowledge that they are afraid to do so. We see failure as the likely outcome simply because so many have failed before us so, we have failed so many time already. When failure as the likely outcome simply because so many times already. When failure and doubt creep into the mind, the war is already lost and that is a when we use our bridge we created in our minds. This is why bridges are so detrimental to our mindset.

CHAPTER TWO

MEN WHO BURNED THIS BRIDGES

Nothing influences the degree of our success more than what expect from us. In short, we get out of life not what we wish, hope or even deserve. We get out of life what we expect.

Of course, it isn't enough just to respect more. We must add hard work, faith; burning desire, persistence, and a positive attitude to the recipe in order to achieve our expectations. But the fact remains, we don't typically get what we deserve, but what we expect. Thus, expectation can either breathe life into us or steal away our Oxygen. When a man exactly desire a thing so deeply that he is willing to stake his entire future on a single turn of wheel in order to get it , he is sure to win

EDWIN C. BARNES

He was the man who determines to work with Edison and he did not achieve it at one sitting. It came little by little, beginning with a burning desire to become a business associate of the great Edison. One of the chief characteristics of Barnes desire was that it was definite. He wanted to work with Edison not for him.

When this desire, or impulse of thought, first flashed into his mind, he was in no position to act upon it. Two (2) difficulties stood on his way. He did not know Edison and he did not have enough money to pay his railroad fair to orange, New Jersey. These difficulties were sufficient to have discouraged the majority of men from making any attempt to carry out the desire but it was not ordinary desire he presented himself at Mr. Edison Laboratory, and announced he had come to go into business with the investor. In speaking of the first meeting between Barnes and Edison years later, Mr. Edison said:-

"He stood there before me looking like ordinary tramp but there was something in the expression of his face which conveys the impression that he was determined to get what he had come after. I gave him the opportunity he asked for, because I saw he had made up his mind to stand by until he succeeds.

Barnes did not get partnership with Edison on his first interview. He did get a chance to work in Edison offices, at a very normal wage.

Month went by apparently nothing happened to bring nearer to converted goal which Barnes had set up in his mind as his definite major purpose. But something important was happening in Barnes mind. The was constantly intensifying his desire to become the business associate of Edison

Barnes was ready for a business association with Edison; moreover, he was determine to remain ready until he got that which he is seeking

He did not say to himself "Ah well, what is the use? I guess I will change my mind and try for a sale man's." but he said " I came here to go into business with Edison and I will accomplish the end if it take the remainder of my life. When the opportunity came, it appeared in a different direction than Barnes had expected. That is one of the tricks of opportunity. It has a sly habit of slip ping in by the back door, and it comes disguised in the form of misfortune, or temporary defeat, perhaps that is why so many fail to recognize opportunity.

Mr. Edison had just perfected a new office device, known at that time as Edison digital machine. His sales men were not enthusiastic over the machine. They did not believe it could be sold without great effort. Barnes saw the opportunity. It had crawled in quietly, hidden in a queer looking machine which interested no one but Barnes and the inventor

Barnes knew he could sell the Edison dictating machine. In fact, he sold it so successfully that Edison gave him a contract to distribute and market it all over the world and himself rich in money

HARRY BANE

Young Harry was frolicking on a playground one day in 1990 when he leaped off a merry-go-round and bumped his leg on a swing set. He and his teacher notice a huge bump on his leg and soon his parents took him to the family doctor. The doctor referred him to a specialist who referred him to yet another Specialist who all pretty much said the same thing! "Should be nothing" one doctor though, hesitated adding; there's a one in a million chance, but ....

Actually, it is closer to a one-in-twenty-five-million-chance- and Harry was that one: he had Adamantinoma, a very rare form of cancers that was eating away at the tibia if his right leg. At the time, only about 250 cases of the disease had been documented.

Harry faced multiple surgeries and who know what else. But he had two huge advantages going into them: a incredible positive mother and father whose optimism and determination left little doubt in his mind that he would survive. As I sat down with them in their home just outside of Boston, Harry's dad, rich recalled:

"I never thought, oh, my God, my kid has Cancer!" instead he said to his wife, Tame, resolved early on that we wouldn't reveal any anxiety to Harry even though they realized he could eventually lose his leg and possibly his life to the disease.

They stressed clear, pragmatic, positive him king, along with the lives of "Okay, that's the situation. Now what are our options? They believed in their heart of heart that every thing was going to be alright.

And when a doctor, a few years later, told them that Harry would have to give up his passion for sport and instead take up violin or chess, his dad shot back, “this kid is going to play sport and be you poster child”

And indeed, he has despite a long and Harry owing serves of setbacks and surgeries, harry who now starred college starred as s little leaguer, was a feisty point gauds in basket ball is a championship golfer, runs and swims. “I wasn’t going to let my leg keep me from playing he said.” I just wasn’t not going to let that happen.

But Young Harry’s determination tested again. He had his first surgery at age seven, when the doctor remove nearly five inches of bone from the labia and replaces it with a metal plate three years later, the replaced his fibula, the smaller of the two lower leg bones with a metal plate inch by inch, piece by piece, little Harry was losing his leg. Two more operation followed graft bone from Harry’s hip into his tibia. And in 2000, surgeons attached a leg straightening device with seventeen metal pins. Each procedure may have dampened Harry’s spirit but nothing could have dampened his resolve. At age twelve, he led his Swampscott, Massachusetts, little league team to the state final. He was startwart at the St. Johns CYO basketball team. And in golf he won his first junior club championship in 1998 and retained the title through 2001, he had what amounted to a broken leg and was wearing his leg straightened. “I didn’t want to be the crippled kid” he said. So when he work he went out for the golf team, he wore long pants and didn’t tell the coach about his leg or ask to use a cart. He made the team, which went undefeated that year.

He also had a terrific sophomore golf season at pingree and thought he was fully recovered. But one day, while playing basketball, he had stolen the ball and was running down the court for an easy lay up when suddenly----SNAP! The next thing he knew was he was lying on the court looking up at his entire team gathered around him. When he looked down, he saw a huge pool of blood on the floor. In shock it took him a few minutes to realize his tibia had snapped in half, and it was sticking out of Tustin.

As if that weren’t enough, his favorite sport basketball, was set it start in just a few days. Harry was the star shorts top, batting third in the line up. Burt instead of suiting up for basket ball practice, he suited up for yet another surgery. Basket ball was out, and his hopes were dashed ones more.

At this point Harry had enough. He wanted to have the doctors amputate his leg and fit him with prosthesis so at least he could play sport. However, his parents would not hear of it. Thee positive attitude was infectious and Harry quickly bounced back as determined as ever.

His dad says Harry is "up" emotionally about 98 percent of the time and "down" only 2 percent. When he hits those low points, Rich and Tame gave him love and affection, but never sympathy. They constantly remind him that no matter how bad he thinks he has it, there are other far worse off than he is.

After the surgery, Harry's leg was wrapped in giant cast, but he wasn't down for long. Less than a month after the cast was removed he captained the US junior team playing against Scotland of stored St. Andrews. Halfway through the ten-day trip, a strange bump appeared on his shin where his tibia had protruded, and discharges of blue, green, red and brown oozed from it. Things didn't look good but they say "The game must go on" he bandaged his leg and kept on playing, wining all his matches, upon returning home, harry discovered that a very bad infection had developed. Fortunately treat it without removing the whole infection bone.

After twelve surgeries in all, Harry says the doctors judge him "Low percent healthy."

ERIK WEITIENMAYER

When Erik Weitienmayer was six month old the doctor learned that he had Retmoschiris, an eye disorder that would slowly destroy his retinas. He grew up knowing he did not have long to see the world, and by the age of thirteen, he was totally blind.

Many people facing such crisis would be gin to pull inward, setting limit on what they could reasonably hope to achieve in life. Not Wehenmayer. He did just the opposite. He pushed outward, expanding his horizons and inflating his dreams. He refused to let his handicap slow him down.

In his thirties, Erik has broken through boundaries few people let alone those who are blind would even dare to approach. He's a marathon runner, skydiver, long distance biker skier, Scuba diver, and member of the college wrestling hall of fame, more amazing yet he's also climbed the three highest mountain in the world and in 2001 achieved his dream of becoming the first blind person to reach the 29,035 foot summit of mount Everest, the world highest mountain.

MARSHALL FIELD

The morning after the great Chicago fire, a group of merchants stood on State Street, looking at the smoking remains of what had been their stores. They went into a conference to decide if they would try to rebuild or leave the Chicago and start over in a more promising section of the country. They reached a decision all except one to leave Chicago.

The merchants who decided to stay and rebuild pointed a finger at the remains of the store and said, "Gentlemen, on that very spot I will build the world's greatest store no matter how many times it may burn down."

That was almost a centaury ago. The store was built. It is called towering monument.

GREAT WARRIOR

A long while ago, a great warrior faced a situation which it necessary for him to make a decision which insured his success on battle field. He was about to send armies on a powerful foe, whose men outnumber his own. He loaded his soldiers into boats, sailed to their enemies country, unloaded the soldiers and their equipments then give order to burn the ship that had carried them. Addressing his men before the first battle he said, you see the boat going up in smoke that means we cannot leave those shores alive unless we win, we have no choice we win or we perish and they won.

SYLESVESTER STALLONE

He was a skinny kid and scort of weird at birth; he'd suffered nerve damage that cost his left eyes and the left side of his mouth to droop. He also had a severe speech impediment and a given name that evoked jeers from other kids in his tough hells kitchen neighborhood.

"Binky" became his nickname, and soon kids were calling him Stinky Binky"

The more he was taunted, the more withdrawn into fantasy world so rich that he sometimes woe a "super boy" costume under his clothes. When a teacher found out she made him strip down the class to show how silly he looked, which obviously did nothing to boost self esteem. He even tried jumping off a roof holding an umbrella, hoping it would help him to fly.

The product of an unhappy home, he changed school fourteen times in just eleven years, his grade were so poor that no one expected him to amount to much. Even military schools couldn't straighten him out. To make maters worse he had a hostile streak that led him to pull pranks so destructive that he seemed a more likely candidate for prison than stardom.

When he was thirteen, Binky saw a movie that will forever change his life. Hercules the main character played by Muscle Man Steve Reeves, inspired him so much that the day after seeing the movie he went to the local junkyard and started lifting weight with old car parts. Later, in college he had minor role in few plays. But he was terrible and receives little encouragement from his instructors.

Still he was determined to become an actor and screen work. So he quit school and went to New York, were he met rejection at every turn.

He lived in a 13-a-week hotel and took odd jobs. Ushering a theater, how king Pizza, mixing salad in deli, selling fish, and even cleaning the lions cage at the zoo. He was broke he had to wash the clothes by wearing them into the shower.

After five years of futilely seeking recognition in New York, he plucked down and 40 for a beat-up old mobile and drove to Hollywood there he got some small acting assignments, and between gigs, he kept to a rigid writing routine, up at dawn seeking to turn the pain of his youth into cinematic goal.

Slowly a glimmer of a story took shape. It was the mid-70s and the nation was emerging from the Vietnam War era. American he reasoned was looking for hope and inspiration for hero. He decided to focus on the stifled ambition and brook on dream of a little person movies goers could identify with and all could root for

His creation, of course, was rocky Balbo the Cinderella like outclassed boxer who becomes a symbolic winner in an epic battle as symbolic champion.

A movie producer was enthusiastic about the scrip and offered him and $75,000 for it. Under the condition that he would not play the lead role. Though he had only $106 in the bank, he said he would not take the offer unless he could play the Rocky.... The producer refused but agreed to raise the offer to $100,000, then $ 330,000! For someone who was so poor that he sold his dog in order t have cash for food, that was insane amount of money. Still he said "No deal" he knows this was the big break he had been searching for. Finally, the producer okayed him for the lead role. But he didn't think the film would do well without a big-name star, so he slashed the films budget and agreed to pay Binky $ 20,000 for the script and $340 per week-minimum wage for the actor.

The movie of course, was Rocky which went on to gross over $160 million and win three academy awards, not to mention spawning a series of highly successful sequels. The writer actor was Sylvester Stallone, who after years of rejection had become an "overnight" sensation at the age of thirty and a creative force to be reckoned with in the movie industry.

Holding tightly onto his dream of playing the lead made all the difference in the world "As far as I am concerned, he said, if I didn't get this part it was the only shot I'd ever get" he was so sure the movie would be a success, he later confessed, that he would have played the part for free.

TAYO AYINLA

He resigned his ₦2, 500 jobs and sold his property for ₦13, 000 and used to start a soap making business. This is how civil engineering graduate became a successful business man.

Like most Nigerian youth, his beginning was rough. Born into a polygamous family, Tayo learnt early in life how to cope with poverty. His parent was poor. His father was working with Philips Nigeria limited, Ojota Lagos. The mother was a sewing mistress and a petty trader. As a child, the family of 16 lived in a room and parlor, ace-me and face you house in Amukoko, Lagos.

But today, the 44-years old man, who graduated as a civil law engineer from the university f Ilorin, is now an employer of labour.

He owns wise trust international limited and Bawoen trust limited a real estate firm in Abuja, he has 103 people, including 6 graduate and 23 professional in his employment, the business has now expanded to estate development, book publishing and training. He is also seven less privileged Nigerians in tertiary institution across the country.

He had started a soup making business with-₦13, 000 after he resigned his appointment with HFP, an engineering firm in Logos. After his mandatory national service with National youth Service in Jos, plateau State, he got a job at HFP engineering is Ikota, Lagos in 1995

"I worked for HFP engineering for one year before I resigned in 1996, "he said "I resigned the work because it exposed me a lot of risks. To be able to join the staff bus, I must be at the bus stop by 5:50am and the bus location is at Moshalasi by a hotel, where you have a lot of hoodlums called area boys who specialize in snatching people's bag and attacking people.

"A day came that I woke up thinking it was 5:30am, rushed to the bus stop as usual and later discovered that I woke up by 3:30 am and not 5:30am. I re-assessed my self that the work is really worth the risk, with nothing to prove to the world that I am working.

Since then, the idea of resign has occupied my mind.

Shortly I went on leave; I resigned the same day I resumed from my leave. I had made up my mind like Esther in the bible, who says if I perish I perish"

"I was not motivated to resign but I was frustrated by the condition of my work that the risk attached to it and the fact that I had nothing to show for my work. My life was caged, in the premises I worked, there I also ate, I receive my salary there. No opportunity or go break outside the office premises and my salary is paid in cash; there is no need to interact with the bank. Then I bought my first television through leverage, payment installments, it was difficult to buy thing on cash" he said

He said after he resigned a job that fetch him ₦2, 500 per month, he went to Mustin to learn soap making. After the completion of the training he started business in a rented apartment.

"I resign from the HFP engineering with nothing but sheer determination and commitment to succeed; I sold some of my household items to raise the sum of ₦13, 000. I went for soup making training in mushim, which is ₦1, 200.

The major challenge faced by him was the mastering act of producing good soup and acceptability of products, ability to get our own market share. He said "to our capital base, we couldn't package our product in paper carton, I used polythene bags latter we bought used cartons and turn it inside out to stamp our name on the plain side.

Another challenge Ajinla faced was lack of vehicle to distribute the products. He latter overcame this when a fraud agreed to sell his used car to him. "I deposited ₦50,

000 for the car and from there, things started to change for better as we were able to market and distribute the products. I was insulted many times, most especially customers who underrate me.

In 2000, Ajinla got married to Roselyn, a HND graduate from Otukpo, Benue state and they relocated to Abuja due to what he called "Devine leading"

At Abuja they got a makeshift structure popularly called "Batcher" and started food vending business. We got an offer to pay the rent of the "Shop" in arrears; we deployed our household cooking utensils with ₦10, 000 to start what we called then, Adonal Kitchen in zone 4, Abuja. We started with three staff I, my wife and a young boy.

"it was tough, the first day we ventured into the food business, we only had enough money to buy garri and some vegetable. We bought ₦100 worth meat and we asked the meat seller to cut it into twelve pieces. The profit of ₦20 was the only thing we went home with

TIM FERRIS

He believed in himself. In fact, he believed so strongly in his abilities that he won the national san shou kickboxing title just six weeks after being introduced to sport.

As a prior all American and judo team captain at Princeton, Tim had worked hard. He was good at his sport but repeated injuries over multiple seasons had continually denied him his dream.

So when a friend called day to invite Tim to watch him in the national Chinese kickboxing championship six weeks away, Tim instantly decided to join him at the competition.

Because he had never been in any kind of striking competition before, he called USA boxing and asked where the best trainer could be found; he travelled to a tough neighborhood in Trenton, New Jersey, to learn from boxing coaches who trained gold medalist. And after 4 gravelling hour a day in the ring, he put in more time conditioning in the weight room, to make up for his lack of time in sport. Tim didn't want to compete, he want to win

When the completion day at last arrived Tim defeated three highly acclaimed opponents before making it to the finals. As he anticipated for what he would have to do before he wins the final match, he closed his eyes and visualized defeating his opponent in the very fist round.

Tim believed and won.

TARIQ IBN ZIYAD

In 711 the famous Iberian general Tariq IBN Ziyad, who actually gave Gibraltar its name decided to invade Spain. He took an army of 7000 Muslims across from northern Africa to southern Spain. Once everybody arrived the commanders asked him what they should do with the ships should they leave a garrison behind to guard them, how should they divide the forces between who stays and guard the ship and who goes forward and conquers Tariq replied "Burn all ships" Tariq knew he was going to be out numbered from the start and so he did not want to dilute his forces and so he created a point of no return. From there it was either conquer or die

HERMAN CORTES

In the early 16th centaury, Spanish conquistador Herman Cortes ventured out on an expenditure to conquer Mexico which was new to European nations. Cortes left on an expedition in direct distance of the Cuban Governor who revoked his charter at the last minute due to an old grape between the two individuals. Nevertheless, Cortes landed Veracruz, Mexico several months later looking to conquer the Aztec Empire and shore, Cortes ordered his men to sink in the fleet of ships to prevent the secretly planned return of Cuba by those loyal to the Cuban Government sinking the ships left the expectation crew no way to retreat. Now they either had to win or perish. Ultimately, Cortes expedition was successful against the Aztecs.

ELLA FITZGERALD

In the 1920s, young Ella had a passion for singing. After her mother's death she would up in a reformatory and sang as a way to escape her harsh reality. Her big chance at a talent contest at Harlem's Apollo Theater. The house was packed and when her name was called, the seventeen-year-old Fitzgerald-homeless, wearing a shabby outfit and men's boots- mustered enough courage to overcome her terrible stage fright and sang-really sang. She won first prize and that night she launched a sixty year singing career she sold more than forty million records and received thirteen Grammy awards.

RUEBEN GONZALEZ

When 20-year-old Rueben Gonzalez showed up at the U.S Olympic training center in lake placid, New York, he had in his pocket the business card of a Houston business man who believed in Olympic dreams. Rueben was there to learn the sport of huge, a sport that 9 of 10 aspirant give up after the first season. Almost-everyone breaks more than one bone before mastering this 90-mile-per-hour race against time in an enclosed mile-long down hill trace of concrete and ice. But Rueben had a dream, passion, and commitment not to quit, and the support of his friend, Craig, back in Houson.

When Ruben got back to his room after the fist day of training, he called up Craig "Craig this is nuts; my side hurts, I think I broke my foot. That is it I am going back to soccer"

Craig interrupted him "Ruben, get in front of a mirror!"

"What"

"I said get in front of a mirror!"

Ruben got up, stretched in front of a full length mirror.

"Now repeat after me! No matter how bad it is and how bad it gets, I am going to make it"

Ruben felt like an idiot starring at himself inside the mirror, so in the most wimpy, wispy, wasty way possible, he said "No matter how bad it is, and how bad it gets, I am going to make it!

"C.mon! say it right, you are Mr. Olympic man! That's all you have ever talked about! Are you going to do it now?"

Ruben started getting serious "No matter how bad it is and how bad it gets, I am going to male it!

Again!

No matter how bad it is and how bad it gets, I am going to male it! And again and again and again about the fifth time Rueben said it, he thought Hey, this feels kind of good. I'm standing a little bit straighter. By the itched time he said it, jumped up in the air and shouted, "I don't care what happens. I am going to make it I can break both legs bones heals I will come back and I will make it I will be an Olympian" Rueben Gonzalez made that declaration, and it changed his life. He went on complete in three separate winter's games in luge-Calgary in 1988, Albertville in 1992 and Salt Lake City in 2002.

JOHN PEPPER

After earning his MBA, John Pepper had little idea what he wanted to do with his life. He opted to go the traditional route and landed a job with a large investment banking company. "I loved the money but absolutely hated the job" he said. He kept telling himself, make the money and then you can do what you love.

But after only six months of "waking and dreading going to work" he could not take it any more and resigned. A voice kept telling him to quit and pursue a restaurant idea he could not stop thinking about. Despite all the friendly advices telling him that he was "throwing away his education and an opportunity to make a lot of money"

Pepper stuck his voices advice. Today, he's the CEO of the wrap, a very successful restaurant chain in Boston area.

LEGSON KAYIRA

As a boy, legson Kayira found it easy to pity himself and to believe that living in a poor village in Africa's Nyasaland (New Malawi) doomed him to a life of want.

But then the school book he read about Abraham Lincoln, a poor man who grew to be a big man arising above his background. "I have never dreamed that there was such a person as poorer than I was" he later wrote "Yet who in the course of his life had accomplished his goal. Go to America and get an education.

Despite having no money, no contacts, and little schooling, in 1958 legson set out to walk to America. "I saw the land of Lincoln as the place where one literally went to get the freedom and independence that one thought and one was due to him". His plan was to walk to Egypt-barefooted, I might add some three thousand miles away, and those to figure out a way to get a ship bound for the United States. His only possessions on his journey were a bible, the pilgrim progress, a small ax, a spare shirt, a blanket, and five days worth food.

Of course, he had no money to pay for his trip to America and no idea which college he would attend, or even if he would be accepted at any school. But he emptied his mind of anything except pursuing his dream of getting an education.

After five days in rough terror, he had covered only twenty-five miles and was out of food. But still trudged, sometimes walking with stranger but often walking alone, between him and his destination were hundred of tribe that spoke more than fifty languages, none of which Legson knew, so he entered each new village cautiously. Sometime he find work and place to stay, but often he camped for forage and food, when times get tough he repeated over and over his school motto: "I will try"

At one point he became gravely ill with fever and more than once he considered returning home. But each time he became discouraged, he read his book and reignited his passion.

Fifteen month after he began his journey, he reached Kampala, Uganda, having covered about a thousand miles. He rested there for a while working odds jobs and indulging in his love of books at the local library. One such book was a directory of junior college in America.

He opened it, and his eyes fell on the listing for Skagit Valley College in Washington State. He decided that was where he would go to school.

Legson wrote Skagit's dean explaining his situation and inquiring about scholarships. The dean was so impressed by the young African determination that he granted him admission to the school as well as scholarship and a job that would pay his room and board. While dated with lay ahead he was aware of the obstacles that lay ahead of he needed a passport, but to get that he needed a verified birth date, which his illiterate parents don't have. As if that was not enough he also needed round-trip airfare before he could even apply for visa.

Without enough money for food and lodging, Legson pushed on believing he would somehow come up with the money. Meanwhile, words of his remarkable odyssey spread, and by the time he reached Khartoum, Sudan-tired, weak and hungry-he learned that Skagit student and local residents there had raise $650 he needed and found him a place to stay in Washington.

In December, 1960 more than two years after he'd began walking, Legson Kayira arrived at Skagit Valley College, still carrying his two treasured books.

Legson graduated from Skagit and continued his education, earning a doctorate from Cambridge University in England, where he later became a political science professor as well as the author of the autobiography (I will try) and four respected novels.

FRANKLIN CHANG-DAIZ

Like many seven-year-old Boys, young Franklin Chang-Daiz dreamed big.

He and his playmate build themselves a spaceship out of a long cardboard box with odd piece of discarded electronic gear for a pilot's seat. They went through a countdown, took off, and landed on a distant planet. For his friends, playing spaceship was just a game; for Chang-Diaz, it represents a dream that he would one day dare to pursue.

He was born into a middle-class family in Costa Rica, and the possibility of his dream coming true seemed about as remote as out or Space itself, given that Costa Rica had no space programme but after the soviet launched sputnik in 1957, his dream took on a new life. He said "a lot of people told me that this was an impossible dream and that people from Costa Rica were not going to be astronauts this was for Americans or Soviet" people told him to get a real job and do something productive with his life. "But" he said "I guess I want not just too interested in listening to that." When he became a teenager, things began to change. For one, his crew disappeared. Most of them realize it wasn't very realistic to keep alive the dream of going into outer space. But by this time, Chang-Diaz knew it wasn't just for childish dream it was his destiny.

He read everything he could get his hands on about space exploration, plastered his walls pictures of space explorers, and dreamed up imaginary spacecraft. When he was fifteen, his eyes lit up when he discovered NASA brochure entitled so you want to be a rocket scientist. He saw his chance and knew he had to act. He wrote a letter to the head of the space agency expressing his enthusiasm, only to make it temporarily quelled by Houston's reply: NASA careers were open only to citizen of the United States

Undeterred Chang-Daiz switched gears- but not his objective. He was not going to accept the limiting life pattern that would keep him in Costa Rica. If NASA career were open exclusively to become one. After graduating in school from Costar Rica, he worked for nine month as a bank teller and saved $50. He then talked his father into buying him a one way plane ticket to the United States. His dad told him, "if you get into trouble just let me know and I will try and get you a return ticket."

"Don't worry about it, you won't need to" the eighteen year-old- replied.

The first leg of his journey began when he arrived in Connecticut with only the $50 in his pocket and an old suitcase stuffed with a few changes of underwear. He was able to live with distant relatives until he adjusted to the strange land "there were times of tremendous doubt" he recalled "after the first few months you feel strong like you can conquer anything-but after a while you realize you are really far away from home, you don't speak the language, you don't have any money. Things were really hard, especially in that first few winters.

At Christmas, a tremendous amount of self doubt hits you al at once. Those were moments when I almost said, "look, I can't do this, I must go back.'

But he didn't do this resisted falling back into the old pattern. He was committed, and it was late to turn back. Although at times it seemed like his dream was on life support, he managed to keep it alive. When I asked him how he managed to pull through hard times he replied, "I was too proud to tell my dad I had given up"

Havens come to the United States without knowing a word of English, he knows he was at a tremendous disadvantage and immersed himself in the new language while attending high school as a senior. Within a year time he went from being the bottom of the class to the top and was thrilled when he was selected for a four year scholarship in the University of Connecticut.

Everything seems on track but another road block threatened his progress. He learned there had been a mistake. The university thought he was U.S citizen from Puerto Rico, not a foreigner from Costa Rica. He wasn't eligible for the scholarship after all.

But Chang-Diaz's determination to go to the college inspired university officials to take his fight to the state legislative, which eventually agreed to make an exception for him. The only catch was that instead of a four years grant, he would receive a stipend for only one year. He gladly accepted and landed a job in a physics laboratory, and worked his way through school.

In 1972 Chang-Diaz took his own "giant step" toward his life long dream when he earned his degree in mechanical engineering. For a poor immigrant from Latin America who only few earlier had come to the United States of America with nothing, this was an amazing accomplishment in and of itself. But he wasn't done yet.

He enrolled in graduating School at M.I.T to learn about cutting edge alternative energy source like fusion research, plasma physics and atomic energy. About the same time finished his PHD, the American space shuttle program with rejuvenated, and he became a fusion physicist at the Araper laboratory in Cambridge, Massachusetts, where the guidance and navigation system for the Apollo missions were built. Occasionally he even saw astronaut at the site and thought, I'm getting closer.

In 1977 Chang-Diaz achieved one of his lifelong dreams: he became an American citizen- and when things really started to pick up steam. NASA announced that it was seeking another team of shuttle astronauts, and he applied. One day in 1980 he was paged at work. "Dr. Chang Diaz" the caller said you have been selected to be a space astronaut. "Do you want the job?"With that one call his twenty-nine years odyssey had finally come full circle. He had just become the first Latin American to ever have bee selected as an astronaut.

CHAPTER THREE

RISK COMES BEFORE REWARD

Burning of bridges starts with risk and ends with reward (Success). Every reward carries a risk; every thing worth doing has a price. If we really desire to become the person we were born to be, we must be willing to accept risk and pay the price, whatever it is whether it's throwing in the towel on a career in order to start a company you've always dreamed about or leaving behind your extended family and friends to move to a paradise you've been living in and get in after it, "nothing ventured, nothing gained." As the saying goes.

It is risky for Howard Schultz to give up his prestigious lucrative sales executive job, sell his house, and move three thousand miles across his country to join a tiny Coffee chain that eventually became Starbucks. It was risky for Amy Tan to leave the doctorate program at U. C. Berkeley against her mother's wishes to pursue her passion for writing. It was risky for mother Teresa to deft the Catholic Church and leave the convent, and breaking the sacred vow in order to help the starving slum dwelling of Calcutta. It was risky for Bill Gates to drop out of Harvard in order to pursue a little-known computer program called DOS.

Where do we get the courage to face up to our fear and take risks?

The answer is in the very essence of our being. Once we discover our gift and uncover our purpose, a paradigm shift occurs in our thinking. Then, and only then, do we begin to understand that the greatest risk is not taking one.

CHAPTER FOUR

GOALS IN THE BRIDGE BURNING

My suggestion:- get into the habit of setting aside twenty minutes everyday to brainstorm, plan, and measure progress toward the achievement of your goals. Place all of your power and energy behind them, especially in the early stages when momentum is curtail. One you are fully committed burn the bridge behind you; leave no possibility of retreat. Cleanse your mind of "contingency planning" or "plan B's" failure cannot be an option here is some other tried and true principles I encourage you to consider:

- Start with a dream. Create a dram that really gets your heart pumping. Use your imagination and see it, hear it, feel it, touch it and taste it.
- Brainstorm and write down your milestones goals:- think of the possible intermediate steps or goals you could accomplish that would lead you one step closer to the achievement of your dream.
- Be precise and establish measurable specifies:- don't say I am going to lose weight" say I am going to lose five pound before the end of the month.
- Set a definite and reasonable schedule:- a goal without a timetable is like a clock without hands, it does not tell you much.
- Put together a written plan:-all travelers in a foreign land need a map to help them navigate. A plan isn't a plan unless it's written.
- Take immediate action:- any time you set a goal, do something-anything-toward its achievement.

GET REASON FOR GOALS

If we aren't passionate about the reasoning behind our goals, we're likely to fail. When we set a goal just because it seems like the thing to do (such as I will make ₦1, 000,000 next year), it lacks the emotional intensity necessary to pull us through the difficult times. And without emotional intensity, we probably won it be energized to give our best and highest performance. Even if we achieve the goal it won't have as much meaning as one that springs from our heart. The reason, the emotion, and the intent behind a goal are what unlocks its power and gives it zest.

Over the years I've found that people are a lot like bicycles. We're fine moving forward. If we slow down and lose our momentum, we are likely to topple over, but if w fist figure out an executing destination, cast our course and keep on pedaling, there is no telling how far our ride take us.

CHAPTER FIVE

THE "NEVER BURN BRIDGE" MYTH

There is a common saying that state that a person "should never burn bridge" this idiom generally means you should not leave a job or relationship on bad terms recklessly. The wisdom is that you should never know when you will need to re-cross the burnt bridge in the future.

The problem with burning you bridge is that you not only have to know you are right, you have to make sure that you will be right in future when you might appreciate the possibility of retreat

As we cannot predict the future, this is obviously impossible, you cannot be sure that you are right about something that hasn't happened. There is always a degree of uncertainty. Also another argument against burning your bridges is that you might all go wrong.

I say so what?

Things do not go wrong in life. Nothing ever goes exactly as planned but always having a safety net will only ensure one thing; that you don't do what you really want to do.

Burning bridges might come with a problem of regret when things go wrong later.

So does that negate the whole practice of burning you bridges your bridges? Of course not if we took attitude, we will never leave the house because we wouldn't even be certain that we would arrive to work safely. It's all about intelligently calculation your risk. What do you think could have happened to Cortes or Tariq if they had burnt their ships?

They might have succeeded anyway or they were aware that they could retreat to safety at any time. Life is not about always being safe.

Without pain, without sacrifice, we would have nothing. Tyler Durden.

Think of all the great men and great things that have been accomplished. Innovations, artistic triumphs, social upheavals, do you think that these things were accomplished by playing it safe? If Thomas Edison were playing it safe he wouldn't have invented bulb and some other things.

CHAPTER SIX

BURNING YOUR BRIDGE-CROSS THE BRIDGE FIRST

Burning your bridge is a tool you can use to help you control your own future actions according to your current beliefs; hence it shouldn't be something you do lightly. Don't burn your bridges before you've crossed them. Burning your bridge does not mean dropping everything at once in the pursuit of your dreams. Dreams have to be worked out intelligently. One step at a time does it. Plan set goals and target work consistently but patiently know how you will got by on the way to achieving your dreams. The important thing is that you never lose sight of your dreams and never give up on them. Burning your bridge however, is not something to be taken lightly. It requires careful thought and reflection. The process of deciding your purpose in life and what you want out of life can be a long one and can take many months and years and even years of refining as you get know yourself better and explore the possibilities life has given you.

But once you reached a point where you know what you want out of life, you need to burn your bridges. You must let go of all other option and pursue the thing that you truly want.

CHAPTER SEVEN

NEGATIVE EFFECT (HAVING OPTION CAN BE A DRAW BACK)

Is there a lack of progress in your life because as soon as you start one thing you drop it and start something else? Can having too much option become a drawback rather than a positive thing?

I will explain three negative effects that too much choice on individuals.

1). CHOICE CAUSES BY ANALYSIS: - deciphering between too many choice is mentally draining and will cause paralysis by analysis instead of liberation. With so many different things to choose from, we find it hard to choose at all. These tough decisions because of excessive choice lead to procrastination. If you speak with many successful people, most will tell you that taking action is the most important part of their achieved success. If you are paralyzed by indecision, there is no way that you can take the action necessary to make you successful.

This phenomena reminds me of some of my genius friends who wander through life because they are good at everything. They have so many good options that they cannot decide which one is the best path for them to take. All of their time is spent striving maximize every decision instead of finding ways to maximize their life. Don't fall into this trap.

2). **CHOICE OF TEMPTATION TO TURN BACK TO ADVERSITY SURFACE:-** Taking a path that leads to happiness and fulfillment can be challenging at times. If not, then every one would be taking that identical path. The split brain that we have makes it difficult to stay on course when adversity surfaces. On one hand, we see our end goal with all the glory in front of us. On the other hand we recognized the hang up that may occur that can negatively affect our self esteem through failure just like Cortes troop almost defected against him, our natural instinct is to turn back when the going gets tough. Power comes from not being able to retreat.

3). **TOO MANY CHOICES OFTEN MAKE US NOT SATISFIED WITH OUR SELECTED OPTION:-** when we keep too many choices on the table for too long we end up less satisfied by our selected option than we could be if we had fewer options instead. How we valued choice depend greatly on the other alternatives that we compare them to. In economics, this called opportunity cost this is cost of forgoing the next best alternative. When we have many options, our mind starts to play trick on us. Instead of comparing the benefits of one option against another, we compare the benefit of our selected options against the combined benefit of all of the other options. Therefore, if the option we pick is not perfect, we become dissatisfied even if the chosen option is wonderful.

A great example of this fact is in relationship; let's say that John has been dating a wonderful woman named Helen for a short period of time. Helen is attractive, intelligent and kind, but she has a laugh that the john find annoying. There is another woman named favor that also likes John. However, John does not find Favor as attractive, intelligent and kind compared to Helen, but favor does not have an annoying laugh. Therefore John would probably decide to stay with Helen.

Now; instead of other suitors let's say John has many women that like him. Instead of comparing Helen as future life mate against each of the girls individually, john creates this super woman in his brain that compares Helen against the attractiveness of Sarah, the intelligent of Amy, and the kindness of Amaka. In essence, creating a person that does not exist. When choice is abundant, this phenomenon is more likely to happen, causing us to Miss out opportunities that may have been better for us.

CHAPTER EIGHT

HOW TO BURN BRIDGE ON YOUR WAY TO SUCCESS

Devotion clarity and believing in yourself. You don't have to be the most talented or the greatest at your craft, but if you have the ambition and the will power to learn and become the best in your respective industry then you will get there. Life is all about how far you wish to take yourself. It's about giving it your all because the moment you don't your bridges and will hold you back unless you get rid of them and have no choice but to succeed.

David Russell says that "the hardest thing to learn in life is which bridge to cross and which to burn. Making this type of decision is difficult"it makes it a combination of acute self awareness and committed action to your selected path. Half hearted involvement will not work. A popular fable explains that "the difference between involvement and commitments is like an egg and ham breakfast the chicken was involved, but the big was committed"

FIVE STEPS TO BURN YOUR BRIDGE

Here are the five steps you need to burn your bridge for success:-

1). DISCOVER YOUR PASSION AND DEVELOP CLARITY OF PURPOSE

Happiness in life not about money and fame, recognition, or even competition. Successful people love what they do and feel compelled to express the best that is within them. They don't strive to be better than their neighbors or contemporaries; they strive to be better than themselves. True genius is created when we discover our gift and express our passion in our profession

> "Learn to get in touch with the silence within your self and know that everything in life has a purpose"

Without a purpose in life it is easy to get side tracked on your life's journey. It is easy to wander and drift, accomplishing little in life. But with a purpose, everything in life seems to be easy to achieve. To be "on purpose" means you are doing what you love to do, doing what you are good at and accomplishing what is important to you. When you are truly on purpose the people, resources and opportunities you need naturally moves toward you. Purpose is a compass that guides you through out. Do not be fooled by common traps that derail many people from the self discovery process. Being in tune with your passion makes it easier to navigate tough life decisions.

"Great mind have purpose, others have wishes"

We can search all over the world for our life's purpose, but it is only when we chose we will actually discover it. Working toward discovering and fulfilling your life's purpose will provide one of the deepest and richest forms when you are truly inspired by the pursuit of your life purpose, dormant forces will awaken within you and carry you to height you never dreamt possible. Whether or not you know it we've each been given a purpose a specific assignment in life. Where you dig to find your gift you are likely to uncover purpose, for jus as an athlete is born with or an artist is born with a creative mind and a patient deposition, you too were born with a gift that told the key to the treasure chest containing your destiny.

2). ELIMINATE THE CHOICES COUNTER TO YOUR PASSION AND PURPOSE

Creating the harmony starts with knowing exactly what you want out of life. Design the life you want in your mind. After you have identified your passion and purpose, you will now need to eliminate the options or discard all other options that do not align with the direction that you want to be in future, no matter how easy the alternative options are. I understand that these steps can be difficult and scary, but it is a necessity.

The human brain is schizophrenia. We constantly have to decide whether to take safe but often unsatisfying route or the tough route that will eventually lead us to our desired destination. When we attempt the tougher path, the safe part of our brain want to multiply against the path and force of retreat of progressive positive action. When facing important, but frightening decisions, it is better to self impose limit on your available choice rather than to keep easy, but unsatisfying choice on more resourceful in overcoming obstacles knowing the retreat is not an option and you be forced to take positive action. There are common trap that entice people not to options that are counter to their passion.

CAREER WORTHINESS

One may think that the unaligned choice is more worthy than the thing that you really want to do. Overcome the urge to think like this. Many people choose "Worthy" careers because they provide an elusion of security, not because they actually like the career. I was a banker which I worked with reputable bank in Nigeria. I resigned to set up my self as an entrepreneur and a writer I want to pursue the path I love and I am sure that I will be successful at it. If you want to be a banker that is excellent, but make sure it is career align with your passion and not because it is deemed. Worthy of others.

BELIEVE IN YOUR SELF:- if you listen solely to the marketing massages on television, it would be easy to feel worthless if you do not own a latest BMW, have an MTV crib, or hang out with latest accessory mate. There is nothing wrong with having these things, but individuals in tune with their purpose will know that these mate relationship will not keep them happy for long.

If you are going to be successful in creating the life dream, you have to believe that you are capable of making it happen you have to believe that you have the right stuff that you are able to pull off. You have to believe in yourself. Believing in yourself is a choice. It is an attitude you develop over time.

It is always funny to hear someone or see some one say you can't do something or give you limitation and explain to you how hard some thing is. Other people like to determine what you cannot do. Don't ever let the exterior world let you down because other people can't determine your will power to get what you want. You can find all the bullshit reasons in to world as to why you can't do something, but is the single thing that is going to keep you where you are in your whole life.

At the end of day it all comes down to belief. It's not how much others believe in you or the limits they place on you. It's based on how much you re willing to take from this world and how hungry you really are. When you tell you're self you can't do something you are creating an illusion in your mind to take you right back over that bridge that you have there as a safety net.

As actors will smith explained in an inspiring interview, having a plan B is only distract from pursuing plan A. in my case, I "Burn the boat" by creating a mission and brand around my number one value. I define freedom lifestyle as the person having the ability to do what he or she wants, when he or she desire. It is an intentional and adventurous way of life, with the individual making a long life commitment of crafting and sharing his or her unique genius (many would say this is foolish, which is OK because I am not speaking to them.) I know that this can be very hard to burn certain bridges. Often there is immersed social pressure to cross the same bridge as everyone else. But ask yourself "who will suffer for my unhappiness if 1 live a life that I do not Love?" the answer is you!

3). TAKE ACTION TO ENSURE YOUR SELECTED ACTION IS IRREVERSABLE

Esteem "nothing happen until something moves" when you bun the bridge the option that are counter productive to your life don't create safety zip lines to take you back "just in case "something goes wrong. The purpose to cutting off the other options is to force ourselves to focus on what we love to do. If you know in the back of your head that you can quit at any time then the focus effect is diminished.

This is the clarity demonstrated by the fact that many of us perennially put off important tasks think of a high school student not doing his homework, a university student not working on his thesis and a working adult not walking on his work project. Each one of these people tell themselves that they will do it tomorrow but when tomorrow becomes today they will take the same action and postpone it to another new tomorrow. This goes on and on until there is little time left and they are forced t take action. The results are usually not that inspiring.

The flip side of thing of our future selves as improved version of our current selves is that we tend to dramatically over estimate how much work we will be able to complete in a given time frame. The problem is that we are not able to know our future selves will have. If you are stressed out no about something, you will probably be stressed out about something else in the future if you haven't got time because you are busy in the present, you will probably also find yourself busy in the future.

Let's imagine you want to write and publish book of poem in two years time. You could just write as it comes to you, but you may spend a lot of time thinking about form. This it self is not a bad thing, but you may find that the givens much choice, you become paralyzed. If you burn a bridge and announced that you will publish a book of Haikus, which is a type of Japanese poem that consist of three lines of five, seven and five syllables.

Suddenly wrote a discussion form is out of the window because you have given yourself a rigid form to adhere to and you can concentrate on getting your massage across our minds love challenge and when you place an unusual constraint on yourself, your mind has to look for unconventional ways to surpass this limitation. The result is that creative flourishes and you gain a new skill.

CHAPTER NINE

THE BENEFIT OF BURNING YOUR BRIDGE

Controlling your in future self:-

Insuring against your future self (discuss that even simple reminders like leaving your running stews by your bed so you remember to pack them away is a form of ensuring against your future self)

The most important and useful benefit of burning your bridge is that you are able to directly control your future self, by limiting your future options, you can insure yourself against any acts "Cowardice" that you future self might suffer. This of course requires a strong believe that you are right. This is extremely useful when you have a tough task to and you set up the conditions which will increase the chance of completing your task.

Forces to prepare you as well as you can:-

You can bet that both Tariq and Cortes didn't take their duties lightly. They were in a life or death situation and so one can imagine the preparation they submitted themselves (and their soldiers) to. Nothing is unnecessary left to chance. If you set yourself up into a situation in which there is no turning back, you can bet you will want to be prepaid for it. It's natural.

Show everyone you mean business:-

The act of burning one bridge may well have been the cause of success; would Cortes have conquered Mexico if he had this flotilla waiting offshore? May be, may be not.

Increase creativity:-

Burning the bridge can actually increase your creativity. While it may appear counterintuitive, it does make sense. Limitations improve creativity by narrowing your field focus and burning a bridge is just another type of limitation. Why does it work? Well it gives you a less to think about. Forcing yourself to make some decision from the onset frees you up to be within the framework

www.ingramcontent.com/pod-product-compliance
Ingram Content Group UK Ltd.
Pitfield, Milton Keynes, MK11 3LW, UK
UKHW041905190726
13854UKWH00003B/1106

9 781312 694941